Table of Contents

D1736753

What Is The Cakes For Cancer Project?

The Cakes For Cancer Project consists of this book, a YouTube Channel (Under the name Chase Sloan) demonstrating cake-decorating techniques and hopefully some merchandise coming soon to raise money for the American Association for Cancer Research (AACR) and Saint Jude Hospital. The project was started by teenage baker and bodybuilder Chase Sloan, an aspiring surgical oncologist who developed a passion for fighting cancer after losing loved ones and learning that so many others had suffered the same fate. In fact, according to the National Cancer Institute, in the US alone, over 606,500 people die from cancer every single year, and many more suffer the pain and uncomfortable treatment that comes with it and debt that may come after.

Chemotherapy treatments currently cost a lot of money, leaving many people struggling to afford treatments that give them a shot at saving their lives, Saint Jude helps families of patients afford care and treats patients with top quality methods, free of charge is needed. Even when patients can afford the treatments worry free, there are still so many advancements that can and need to be made. Many people, including scientists still don't know much about cancer and it must be researched to save more lives. This is what the American Association for Cancer Research (AACR) helps with by funding research studies and fellowships for physicians and scientists. Therefore, The Cakes for Cancer Project hopes to make even the smallest dent in the amount of people who suffer from cancer by helping to fund groundbreaking cancer research and treatment for those who need it. Thank you so much for purchasing this book and know that anyone can make a difference, even if it seems so small and that together, our small efforts can help to end cancer.

About This Book

This book is in memorial of and was inspired by Anne Duli. Who was Anne Duli, you may ask? She never made the history books, but she was and did so many amazing things. For starters, she was a financial administrator at the Case Comprehensive Cancer Center of Case Western Reserve University, where she managed multiple employees who respected and looked up to her. She was "the person to go to when anything needed to get done" and welcomed others with open arms. Outside of work, she was a proud married lesbian and advocated for equality for all by working with the Human Rights Campaign alongside her loving wife of 20 years, Ana.

Together, the two of them were also caring mothers to many dogs from whom they were almost inseparable. Anne's passion for these animals was truly one of many testaments to how caring and patient of a person she was. Her nickname was ironically 'Bobcat' due to her energetic, perseverant spirit in and out of the house. She was truly an amazing woman with an outstanding problem that not even she could overcome or wait out….widespread cancer. She was a fighter and survived a rough case of breast cancer in the 1980s and another one in 2001. But, when the cancer returned all over her body in 2017, it eventually became more than her doctors could handle and, after 2 years of fighting and holding on, in the summer of 2019, she sadly passed away.

There are many things I remember Anne by, but one of the best memories I have is cooking with her. She was an Italian by birth, and, with that, a meticulous chef who ran a tight home kitchen and loved the details of cooking, but, most importantly, she made amazing food full of passion and family history. Cooking with her and for her was a truly magical and inspiring (yet tedious at times) experience that I will never forget. One of her mottos was to make food that made people smile, and even if it took lots of time and energy, that would be worth it. Therefore, I wholeheartedly dedicate this cookbook to her, in honor of filling the world with more delicious, homemade food to bring people together.

Cakes

Vanilla Cake

Sometimes the best things are the simplest and a good vanilla cake almost always hits the spot, even for those who are cake naysayers! Ironically, my mom, known as an extreme chocoholic is generally not a fan of chocolate cake! She typically only eats the frosting off cakes, which makes her a match made in heaven for my dad who doesn't like icing. However, after noticing that she *would* occasionally eat some vanilla cake, I decided that I was going to try and make her love cake as much as I do with the ultimate vanilla cake recipe. Surprisingly, unlike most of my schemes to make my mom change her mind, this worked! She will actually eat whole pieces of this cake along with the frosting, and enjoy it. We agree that the keys here are having the an oil based cake, which makes it extra moist and adding vanilla bean paste with actual flecks of vanilla in, which goes a long way in amping up the often considered simple and boring vanilla flavor.

Ingredients:

-3 cups flour

-1 cup oil

-3 eggs

-⅔ cup sour cream or plain yogurt

-2 ½ tsp vanilla extract

-2 cups sugar

-¾ cup milk

-2 tsp baking soda

-1 ½ tsp baking powder

Steps:
1. Add the eggs and sugar into a small bowl and beat until pale and fluffy.
2. Add the sour cream or yogurt into the egg and sugar mixture and beat to combine.
3. Slowly pour in the oil while beating to emulsify the mixture.
4. Pour in the vanilla extract, baking powder and baking soda and mix to combine.
5. Add in half of the flour and mix until just combined.
6. Add in the milk and mix to combine.
7. Add in the rest of the flour and mix until combined.
8. Divide the batter between 2 greased 9 inch round pans and bake at 350 degrees Fahrenheit for about 40 minutes.

Chocolate Cake

One of the recipes I am most proud of, and love to eat the most, this cake is the combination of everything I have loved about other chocolate cake recipes I have made over the years rolled into one. I have always been a chocolate cake connoisseur, if you will, so having a perfectly rich, moist, tender chocolate cake in my arsenal was a must and this recipe is it! The heavy hand on the cocoa powder (á la Hershey's), combined with the use of butter rather than oil for flavor and lift (á la King Arthur Flour), stacked on top of the tiny bit of espresso to enhance the chocolate (,a la Ina Garten) is the triple threat that makes this cake irresistible.

Ingredients:
- 1 ¾ cups flour
- 1 cup salted butter, softened
- 3 eggs
- 1 ¾ cups sugar
- ¾ cup plus 2 tbsp cocoa powder
- 1 tsp ground coffee
- 1 cup boiling water
- 1 tsp baking soda
- 1 ½ tsp baking powder
- ⅓ cup milk

Steps:
1. Cream together the sugar and butter until fluffy.
2. Add the eggs one by one, mixing until each one is fully incorporated.
3. In a separate cup or bowl, add the cocoa and coffee to the water and mix until fully combined.
4. Add the cocoa mixture to the butter and sugar mixture and mix.
5. Add in the baking powder and baking soda.
6. Add in half of the flour and mix until incorporated.
7. Add in the milk.
8. Add in the remaining flour.
9. Pour ½ of the batter into each of 2 greased 9 inch round pans.
10. Bake at 350 degrees Fahrenheit for 35-40 minutes or until a toothpick comes out clean.

Lemon Blackberry Swirl Cake

Mastered the vanilla and chocolate cakes? Want to step it up a notch? Try this flavor-packed cake! Almost everybody I know loves strawberry lemonade. Yet, there are other berries out there that pair very well with the tartness of lemon, and this cake is for sure a fun way to showcase that. The sweet, homemade jam adds a great flavor mixed into the layers of the lemon cake and a gorgeous spiral of color! The layers of these caked look awesome even when un-iced and are a pretty sly way to impress a crowd with a very fancy- looking confection.

Ingredients:

  For the cake batter:
-1 tablespoon plus 1 teaspoon fine lemon zest (3-4 lemons' worth)
-½ cup plus 1 tbsp lemon juice
-1 cup oil
-2 cups sugar
-1 teaspoon vanilla extract
-4 eggs
-⅔ cup milk
-3 ¼ cups flour
-3 tsp baking powder
-1 tsp vanilla extract

  Blackberry jam:
-3 tbsp water
-6 oz blackberries
-⅓ cup sugar
-1 tsp lemon juice

Steps:
1. Put the jam ingredients into a saucepan over medium-low heat.
2. Stir and mash the mixture until the sugar is fully dissolved and the berries break down.
3. Continue to simmer the mixture until they fully break down and the mixture begins to reduce, about 8-12 minutes.
4. Set aside the jam in a small bowl.
5. Begin to make the cake batter; cream the eggs and sugar in a large bowl until smooth and well-combined.
6. Slowly pour in the oil while mixing and beat until fully incorporated.

7. Pour in the lemon juice and zest, vanilla and baking powder and mix again until combined.
8. Alternate adding ⅓ of the flour and ½ of the milk and mixing until all the ingredients are formed together.
9. Divide the batter between 2 greased 9 inch round cake pans and set aside
10. Dollop some jam into each pan of cake batter, use a toothpick to swirl the jam but do not incorporate it fully.
11. Bake the cakes at 350 degrees Fahrenheit for 32-38 minutes or until a toothpick inserted into the middle emerges clean.

Red Velvet Cake

The flavor of this classic Southern cake is subtle, but unique. The buttermilk and hint of cocoa (this recipe uses a bit more than most for a richer flavor) combine in a way that gives a not-too sweet and ultra-moist flavor and texture that is pretty hard to resist….even if you don't like the color red. Yes, this cake is meant to be red and the chemical reaction of the cocoa and buttermilk gives the batter a red hue even before it is dyed, but, the first time I made this recipe for other people after writing and testing, I had to make it green! Why green? The cake was a birthday cake for my younger cousin, Sadie, who has a passion for green like no other person I've known, and she wanted a green cake with green frosting and green decorations. The cake ended up looking great, especially for my first two-tier cake. It was daunting, but, it was her tenth birthday and I wanted to make it extra special. Of course, it was *very* green inside and out between the cake, white chocolate mousse filling dyed green and green buttercream. To top it off, I even used green candies melted then broken to look like glass and hand-piped chocolate letters. Not what you imagine when you think of red velvet, but it was what she wanted, so it happened!

Ingredients:
-1 ¾ cups sugar
-1 ⅓ cup buttermilk
-2 ½ cups flour
-½ cup cocoa powder
-1 tsp white vinegar
-1 tsp vanilla extract
-3 large eggs
-1 ½ tsp baking powder
-¾ tsp baking soda
-1 cup vegetable oil
-3-4 drops food coloring of choice

Steps:

1. In a large bowl, cream together the eggs and sugar until slightly pale and smooth.
2. Add in the oil and mix until fully incorporated.
3. Add in the vinegar, vanilla, baking powder and baking soda, mix to combine.
4. Add in the cocoa powder and ⅓ of the flour and mix until just incorporated and then add ½ of the buttermilk, mix, and repeat the process until all the ingredients are incorporated.
5. Divide the batter between 2 greased 9 inch round pans and bake at 350 degrees Fahrenheit for about 35 minutes or until a toothpick comes out clean.

Marble Cake

A favorite of mine since the grocery store birthday cakes of my early years, marble is just plain awesome any way you slice it. Literally, any way you slice it you get both chocolate and vanilla cake in every bite for a mouthful loaded with flavor. My grandma originally taught me to make marble cake with vanilla boxed mixes by adding cocoa powder to about 1/3 of the batter and swirling it in. This recipe plays off that technique,, but for the sake of having a super strong, rich chocolate batter to stand out next to the vanilla, this recipe uses both cocoa powder and melted chocolate which gives it a prominent fudgy flavor.

Ingredients:
-3 cups flour
-1 cup salted butter, softened
-3 eggs
-½ cup sour cream or plain yogurt
-2 tsp vanilla extract
-2 cups sugar
-5 oz semisweet chocolate, melted and cooled
-4 tbsp cocoa powder
-1 cup milk
-2 tsp baking soda
-1 ½ tsp baking powder

Steps:
1. Add the butter and sugar into a small bowl and cream until smooth and fluffy.
2. Add the eggs one by one, mixing before adding the next egg.
3. Add the sour cream or yogurt into the egg, butter and sugar mixture and beat to combine.
4. Pour in the oil while beating, slowly to emulsify the mixture.
5. Pour in the vanilla extract, baking powder and baking soda and mix to combine.
6. Alternate adding in ⅓ of the flour and ½ of the milk and mix between each step until just combined.
7. Remove 2 cups of the vanilla batter and add in the chocolate and cocoa, mix to incorporate.
8. Divide the vanilla batter between 2 greased 9 inch round pans and then dollop the chocolate batter into the vanilla. Use a toothpick to swirl them together to create the marbled look.
9. Bake at 350 degrees Fahrenheit for about 35-40 minutes.

Pumpkin Cake

As I have gotten older and busier with school and other hobbies like bodybuilding, I have developed a bit of a bad habit of forgetting when I put cakes in the oven, occasionally overbaking them. Thankfully, I loaded this recipe with both yogurt and pureed pumpkin which makes it super moist and tender and keeps it that way, even if I spend a few more minutes than intended in the gym and pull it out a bit late. I have made this cake for everything from birthdays to Rosh Hashanah to late summer BBQs and it is almost always a hit. Likely because it pretty much tastes like fall should taste with sweetness, spiciness and lots of pumpkin!

Ingredients:
- 15 oz pumpkin purée
- 3 cups flour
- 1 ¼ cup sugar
- ⅓ cup plus 1 tbsp packed light brown sugar
- 3 eggs
- ¾ cup salted butter, softened
- ½ cup unflavored yogurt
- ⅓ cup milk
- 2 tsp baking powder
- 1 tsp baking soda
- 1 ¾ tsp cinnamon
- ¾ tsp nutmeg
- ¼ tsp ground cloves
- ½ tsp ground ginger

Steps:
1. In a large bowl, combine the butter and sugars and beat until smooth.
2. One by one, add in and incorporate the eggs.
3. Add in the spices, yogurt, pumpkin, and leaveners and mix again.
4. Add in 2 cups of flour and mix to combine.
5. Add in the milk and mix again.
6. Add in the remaining flour and mix until fully incorporated.
7. Pour the batter into 2 greased 9 inch round pans and bake at 350 degrees Fahrenheit for around 40 minutes to an hour or until a toothpick comes out clean.

Almond Cake

Sweet, nutty and mellow...the ideal family dog's traits, right? This cake, though similar in taste to a lot of wedding cakes, was actually something I first made while just messing around with random things in the kitchen after my family adopted our first dog, Duke. Staying home and playing with him was my number one priority. But, as I soon learned, puppies nap a lot so while he slept, I baked. The first thing I found while searching for unique things in the pantry was almond extract, which I had worked with a few times but never in cake. Making the batter perfect with a prominent, but not overpowering, almond flavor and texture took a lot of tasting and smelling. Thankfully, I had both my parents home to help, and soon enough, the recipe was done and cake was in the oven.

Ingredients:
-2 cups all-purpose flour
-1 cup fine blanched almond flour
-1 ½ cups sugar
-1 ¼ tsp almond extract
-2 tsp vanilla extract
-1 cup salted butter, melted
-3 eggs and 1 egg white
-2 tsp baking powder
-1 tsp baking soda
-1 cup milk

Steps:
1. In a large bowl, combine the eggs, egg white and sugar and beat until smooth and light in color.
2. Add in the butter slowly, mixing to incorporate.
3. Add in the leaveners and extracts and mix to incorporate fully.
4. In a separate bowl, whisk together the flour and almond flour.
5. Add half of the flour mixture to the wet mixture and mix to combine.
6. Add in the milk and mix to incorporate.
7. Add in the remaining flour and mix until fully incorporated.
8. Bake the cake in greased 9 inch pans at 350 degrees Fahrenheit for about 30-40 minutes.

Pineapple Cake

One of many recipes for cake created for a specific person, this one was made for Anne's wife, Ana. A proud Puerto Rican, she loves all tropical fruit flavors and has been a huge cheerleader for me throughout my baking endeavors, so I had to make something special for her birthday. Ana has never been a fan of artificially flavored things and neither am I so, including real pineapple in not one but two forms, the juice and puree were musts here. All the fresh fruit also gives the cake a moist stickiness that is almost reminiscent of pineapple upside down cake!

Ingredients:
-3 cups flour
-1 ⅓ cups sugar
-2 eggs
-10 tbsp salted butter, softened
-1 cup pineapple juice
-¾ cup pineapple purée
-1 ½ tsp baking soda
-2 tsp baking powder
-½ tsp vanilla extract

Steps:
1. Beat the butter and sugar until light and fluffy.
2. Add in the eggs one by one, mixing until combined between additions.
3. Mix in the pineapple purée, vanilla, and leaveners until fully combined.
4. Add in half of the flour and mix until incorporated.
5. Add in the pineapple juice and mix until incorporated.
6. Add in remaining flour and mix until fully combined.
7. Pour into 2 greased 9 inch round pans and bake at 350 degrees Fahrenheit for 40-45 minutes.

Angel Food Cake

Angel food cake sounds like what it is, light, airy and compatible with pretty much any other flavor. I love filling it with berry compote, mousse and ganache, or even caramelized apples and finishing it off with a torched marshmallow meringue icing, but you can truly pair it with almost anything. This recipe, unlike many others, uses a fair amount of vanilla extract just to have some flavor other than egg whites (I eat too many of those to count anyways, I don't need cake to taste like them too). Nonetheless, it still has just a subtle hint of it and a mild sweetness that is begging to have a unique flavor added to its impeccable texture.

Ingredients:
-1 cup flour, sifted
-12 large egg whites
-1 ⅓ cups sugar
-¼ tsp salt
-2 tsp vanilla extract
-1 ½ tsp cream of tartar
-3 tbsp water

Steps:

1. In a food processor, pulse the sugar until it is extremely fine and then combine half of it with the flour and salt.
2. In a separate bowl, whip the egg whites, vanilla, water, and cream of tartar until soft peaks begin to form.
3. Slowly add the rest of the sugar into the egg whites and continue to whip until stiff peaks form.
4. Gently fold half of the flour mixture at a time into the egg white mixture.
5. Add the batter to 2 greased 9 inch round cake pans and bake at 350 degrees Fahrenheit for about 35 minutes or until a toothpick comes out clean.

Peppermint Cake

If I'm being completely honest, I've never been a huge fan of anything peppermint, and this cake was actually a mission for me to make myself get the hype behind the classic holiday flavor and make something great out of it. I knew going in that I wanted this cake to be light, since mint is generally a refreshing, fragrant flavor, and I wanted it to shine without being too much. That's where the combo of eggs and whites and the more generous use of baking powder to soda come in. The resulting texture to me is somewhere between an angel food cake and a standard white cake which pairs well with the subtle peppermint flavor from the extract, there's only 1 tsp of it but, as I learned in a few first tries of this, a little extract goes a long way!

Ingredients:
- 2 ⅔ cup flour
- 1 tsp peppermint extract
- 2 tsp baking powder
- ½ tsp baking soda
- ½ cup sour cream or Greek yogurt
- 1 cup salted butter, softened
- 2 eggs plus 2 egg whites
- 1 ¾ cups sugar
- 1 cup milk

Steps:
1. Combine butter and sugar in a bowl and beat until fluffy.
2. One by one, add the eggs and egg white and beat for 5 minutes or until light and airy.
3. Add in the sour cream, peppermint extract, and leaveners and mix to combine.
4. Add ⅓ of the flour, then ½ of the milk, mixing in between and repeat until all the ingredients are mixed together.
5. Divide between 2 greased 9 inch round pans and bake at 350 degrees Fahrenheit for 35-45 minutes or until cooked through.

Banana Cake

This cake was literally made for my dad. He is a big-time banana bread lover and would normally be fine just slicing up a loaf and enjoying it but, I felt that, for father's day, I wanted to do something a little more special than just a simple loaf cake to show him how much I truly care and appreciate him. So, I was faced with a puzzle, how to make banana bread into a layer cake? It may seem simple, but most banana breads are denser than cake, making them not ideal to bake in round pans and layer. Hence, I got to work and attempted to make a cake with the same flavor and moisture of banana bread, but with a little more lift to ensure it baked well and wasn't too dense when stacked. I took a bit of a risk by baking the new recipe for the first time on the actual occasion, but thankfully, it turned out super well. It both looked and tasted great when iced up in chocolate frosting and toasted coconut (another favorite of my dad's)!

Ingredients:
-3 cups flour
-3 ripe bananas
-3 eggs
-1 ⅔ cup sugar
-1 ¾ tsp vanilla extract
-¾ cup melted salted butter
-⅔ cup Greek yogurt
-2 tsp baking powder
-1 ¼ tsp baking soda
-⅔ cup milk
-1 tsp cinnamon

Steps:
1. Mash the bananas in a large bowl, add the eggs, and whisk until combined
2. Add the butter and sugar and beat until light and airy
3. Add in the Greek yogurt, vanilla, leaveners and cinnamon and mix to combine
4. Add in half of the flour and mix until combined
5. Add in the milk and mix until combined
6. Add in the remaining flour and beat to incorporate fully
7. Pour the batter into 2 greased 9 inch round cake pans and bake at 350 degrees Fahrenheit for 35-40 minutes

Classic Carrot Cake

Carrot cake will always have a special place in my heart. The reason being that the recipe here is basically just an amped-up and even more moist version of a carrot cake recipe from my great grandma which has been the staple at my family's Thanksgiving dinners for as long as I remember. For the longest time, it was something that we *only* made for Thanksgiving, which just made me look forward to it like crazy and crave it more. Now, this cake has become so popular among our family and close friends that it is requested year-round, and I gladly make it without thinking twice. Of course, we still make it every Thanksgiving as well, and I am honored to have my cake at a spot on the dessert table.

Ingredients:
-2 ¾ cup all-purpose flour
-1 ½ cup light brown sugar
-½ cup plus 2 tbsp sugar
-2 ¼ tsp baking powder
-½ tsp baking soda
-1 ¾ tsp cinnamon
-½ tsp nutmeg
-4 eggs
-1 tbsp molasses
-½ tsp ground ginger
-1 ⅓ cup vegetable oil
-½ cup milk
-2 ½ cups grated carrots

Steps:
1. Put the eggs, oil, molasses and sugars in a large bowl and mix until the color lightens and the mixture is smooth.
2. Add in the spices and 1 ½ cups of flour and mix until combined.
3. Pour in the milk and mix until combined.
4. Fold in the last 1 cup of flour.
5. Divide the cake batter between 2 greased 9 inch round pans and bake at 325 degrees Fahrenheit until a toothpick comes out clean (about 40 minutes).

Grapefruit Ginger Cake

Both strong, love it or hate it flavors, grapefruit and ginger team up in this cake to create a fresh, citrusy flavor. The story of this recipe is sort of a funny one, in that it was simply just me wanting to create a super unique cake that intrigued people at its mention. Obviously, I wanted to make something that tasted good despite its out of the box-ness, and after eating grapefruits with my dad and my dog, Duke, for many nights after dinner, inspiration struck. After brainstorming a very long list of things that might go with grapefruit, I remembered how much I love ginger in sweets and noticed that I didn't yet have a recipe for it, hence grapefruit ginger cake was born!

Ingredients:
- ¾ cup salted butter, softened
- ½ cup grapefruit juice
- 1 tbsp fine grapefruit zest
- 1 ½ cups sugar
- ¼ cup dark brown sugar
- 2 tbsp grated fresh ginger
- 3 eggs
- ¾ cup milk
- 2 ¾ cups flour
- 2 tsp baking soda
- 1 tsp baking powder

Steps:
1. In a large bowl, cream together the butter, ginger, grapefruit zest and sugars.
2. Add in the eggs one by one, mixing in between additions.
3. Pour in the grapefruit juice and mix once more.
4. Add in the leaveners and ⅓ of the flour, then ½ of the milk, and repeat, mixing between each step.
5. Divide the batter between 2 greased 9 inch round cake pans and bake at 350 degrees Fahrenheit for 35-40 minutes.

Chocolate Spice Cake

This cake was actually inspired by a cookie! As a birthday gift, my mom ordered me some half pound cookies from New York City to try and one of them was a dark chocolate spice base with chocolate chips. I completely fell in love with the warm, and spicy flavor combined with the rich, melty chocolate and immediately wanted to try and recreate it as a cake. After much trial and error, (and I mean like *big* error, as in blow your mouth off spicy cakes) and a few taste tests gone wrong, this cake was born, and it was for sure worth the work.

Ingredients:
-2 cups flour
-3 eggs
-1 ½ tsp chili powder
-2 tsp cinnamon
-1 ¾ cups sugar
-¾ cup cocoa powder
-1 cup oil
-1 cup plus 2 tbsp boiling water
-1 tsp baking soda
-1 ½ tsp baking powder
-⅓ cup milk

Steps:
1. Cream together the sugar and eggs until pale and smooth.
2. Add in the oil slowly and mix until fully incorporated and emulsified.
3. Add the cocoa and spices to the water and mix until fully combined.
4. Add the cocoa mixture to the butter and sugar mixture.
5. Add in the baking powder and baking soda.
6. Add in half of the flour and mix until incorporated.
7. Add in the milk.
8. Add in the remaining flour.
9. Pour ½ of the batter into each of 2 greased 9 inch round pans.
10. Bake at 350 degrees Fahrenheit for 35-40 minutes or until a toothpick comes out clean.

Key Lime Cake

Longing for a taste of a Floridian vacation? This is the cake for you. The sweet, tart and very zesty flavor of this cake reminds me of eating key lime pie on Captiva Island for spring break with my parents. Whenever we go to a restaurant there that has key lime pie on the menu, it is almost an unwritten rule for us to order a slice and have at least one little bite, so on the flight home, we can reflect and argue over which one was best. I originally started working on this cake fresh off a Florida trip and missing that key lime flavor like crazy, so rest assured that it can cure those key lime pie cravings almost as well as the pie itself.

Ingredients:

-½ cup plus 1 tbsp lime juice
-4 tsp fine lime zest
-2 cups sugar
-1 cup salted butter, softened
-1 tsp vanilla extract
-1 cup milk
-½ cup sour cream or Greek yogurt
-3 eggs
-3 cups flour
-1 tsp baking powder
-2 tsp baking soda

Steps:

1. Cream the butter and sugar into a small bowl until light and fluffy
2. Add the eggs one by one, beating between each addition
3. Add in the Greek yogurt/sour cream and mix to combine
4. Pour in the lime zest and juice, vanilla extract, baking powder and baking soda and mix to combine
5. Add in half of the flour and mix until just combined
6. Add in the milk and mix to combine
7. Add in the rest of the flour and mix until combined
8. Divide the batter between 2 greased 9 inch round pans and bake at 350 degrees Fahrenheit for about 40 minutes

Lighter Flourless Chocolate Cake

Being a bodybuilder and a baker is tough, often times, I can't eat what I make or can only eat very small amounts of it to stay on my diet plan. Most days, I'm totally fine eating a small slice or just one cookie, but sometimes I want a gigantic piece of something rich and satisfying and don't want to feel guilty, hence I created! Greek yogurt and egg whites do the heavy lifting here, adding moisture, lift and protein while the combination of real sugar and sugar free Truvia blend adds a good sweetness without overdoing the added sugar. The dark chocolate ties everything together with its rich flavor and also adds some antioxidants!

Ingredients:

-9 oz dark chocolate (about 65%)
-3 eggs and 3 egg whites
-½ cup butter or coconut oil
-⅔ cup low-fat Greek yogurt
-½ cup cocoa powder
-½ cup sugar
-4 tablespoons plus 1 tsp Truvia

Steps:
1. Melt together your butter and dark chocolate in a microwave in 30 second intervals, making sure to not let the chocolate burn.
2. Separate your eggs, setting the whites in a large mixing bowl off to the side.
3. Add the sugar, Truvia, yogurt and cocoa powder into the chocolate and butter mixture and whip for a few minutes until smooth and cooled.
4. Add in the egg yolks and whisk to combine.
5. Beat the egg whites until stiff peaks form.
6. Gently fold in a large dollop of egg whites into the rest of the ingredients.
7. Start adding more egg whites and folding until the mixture is complete.
8. Bake at 350 degrees Fahrenheit for about 40-45 minutes in a greased and cocoa powdered 9-inch round springform pan lined with foil to prevent leakage which has been submerged in a 1 inch water bath.

Frostings and Drizzles

Classic Vanilla American Buttercream

The most simplistic buttercream in the books, vanilla American style frosting is super easy to make and pair with any cake. So many times, delicious looking pieces of vanilla-frosted cake look delicious, but you bite into them only to find the icing is sickeningly sweet and barely tastes of vanilla…with this recipe I say, "Not today!" The use of salted butter has been called unconventional by many people I know, especially my grandmother, but it ensures that the buttercream has that counterbalance of salt to sugar and minimizes ingredients, to me, that's a win! Also, the vanilla bean paste here really does bring it over the top and add the amazing scent and flavor of real vanilla, recognizable even before you dig in because of those little seeds. This recipe may be for a basic thing, but the result is beyond basic for sure.

Ingredients:
-1 ½ cups salted butter at room temperature
-3 cups powdered sugar
-1-2 tbsp milk
-1 tsp vanilla extract
-2 tsp vanilla bean paste

Steps:
1. Add the butter and 1 ½ cups of powdered sugar to a bowl and beat until combined.
2. Add the remaining powdered sugar and the milk and beat once more until combined.
3. Add in the vanilla extract and paste and mix until combined.

Vanilla Swiss Meringue

It takes more time and effort, but it's the official frosting of most professional bakeries so having a meringue frosting in your arsenal is a must. The texture of this stuff is impeccable, super light and melt-in-your mouth, yet sturdy enough to decorate cakes beyond your wildest dreams. After learning and failing to make meringue on multiple occasions and using other recipes, I developed this one, which is heavy on the vanilla flavor and egg whites for a smooth, extra light, flavorful icing on any cake. Don't get me wrong, this one is a bit time-intensive, and if you don't have an automatic stand mixer, it's a full-on arm workout. Still, the result is worth the extra work and the ability to show somebody you care that will come with it.

Ingredients:
- 6 egg whites
- 1 ⅔ cups sugar
- ½ cup water
- 1 ¼ cup salted butter at room temperature
- 1 tbsp vanilla bean paste or vanilla extract

Steps:
1. Whisk the egg whites and sugar in the bowl of a stand mixer over a double boiler
2. When the egg mixture reaches 160 degrees Fahrenheit, take it off the heat and put it under the mixer
3. Whip the mixture for about 15-25 minutes until it is light and glossy and has **fully** come to room temperature (check by placing your hand against the side of the bowl)
4. Cut the butter into tablespoon-sized pieces and add them one by one into the egg white mixture, beating continuously until all the butter is incorporated and the buttercream is light and fluffy
5. Mix in the vanilla until fully incorporated
6. Whip the frosting for 2-3 additional minutes to add extra air

Whipped Chocolate Frosting

Though I can't really imagine why, my little cousin, Stella, has always had an enormous love for grocery store buttercream frosting. So much so, that at one point, she didn't even want me to make her a birthday cake, she wanted one from the store! I was determined to make an equally light and fluffy, yet more flavorful version that would win even her over, so I got to work. After a surprisingly small amount of research, I found that the secret was in the shortening (100% fat with minimal other flavor)! With my new knowledge, I confidently told Stella that I could make a "super duper like really fluffy frosting," and she agreed to let me bake her cake for her. I was ecstatic and made the mistake of asking a nine-year-old what kind of cake she wanted, the answer was…. Poop emoji. I wasn't about to let her down, though…after all, one only gets limited chances to make a poop cake, so I decided to have fun with it. That's how this impeccably fluffy, sweet, chocolaty and brown frosting came to be, yet it is still a family favorite (even compared to grocery store versions) for its great flavor.

Ingredients:
-2 sticks salted butter at room temperature
-1 cup shortening
-5.3 oz Greek yogurt
-5 cups powdered sugar
-¾ cup plus 2 tsp cocoa powder

Steps:
1. Add the butter, Greek yogurt and shortening to a bowl and beat to combine
2. Add the cocoa powder and 1 ½ cups of powdered sugar to the mix and beat until incorporated
3. Add the remaining powdered sugar and the milk and beat once more until fully combined

Cream Cheese Frosting

This one may only be five ingredients, but what a magical combination of five things it is. A frosting good and flavorful enough to eat on its own, this cream-cheese-heavy version of a classic Southern frosting tastes to me like a sweeter, thinner cheesecake batter and that is for sure not a bad thing. It was a no brainer for me to make this recipe more cream cheese-centric than most other recipes you'll find, but that gives it a prominent tang and impeccable richness that even my dog, Duke, loves. He may not be the toughest food critic, but he clearly loves this stuff because he once broke a record two-month streak of not stealing food off the counter to lick this frosting off a cake's sides. Of course, I was too busy laughing to be mad, and I hold no grudges on him. Just a warning though, if you have a dog around, you may want to watch this frosting closely.

Ingredients:
-24 oz cream cheese
-1 cup softened salted butter
-1 ½ tsp vanilla extract
-1 ½ tsp vanilla paste
-5 ½ cups powdered sugar

Steps:
1. In a bowl, combine the butter and cream cheese until a cohesive mixture is formed.
2. Add in the vanilla and mix until incorporated.
3. Add the powdered sugar cup by cup and mix until smooth, adding milk as needed.

Berry Coulis

Almost quite literally the icing on the cake since it a drizzle *on the icing on the cake,* this has become one of my favorite ways to add a pop of bright color and fresh, tart, fruity flavor to cake, tarts or other confections in need of a little extra wow factor. One of my favorite things about this recipe and the reason there are no frills on it besides a little lemon for balance of sweetness is that it can be made with any berry or even a combo of many! Some of the times this has come out the best for me is when I've actually just dumped a bunch of overripe berries into the pot and made treasure of what may have been trash in mere days. I am all about minimizing food waste and recycling soft berries with a coulis is a delicious (I wish I could also call it nutritious) way to do that.

Ingredients:
-2 ½ packed cups berries of your choice
-⅔ cup plus 1 tbsp sugar
-2 tbsp lemon juice
-1 tbsp lemon zest
-⅔ cup water

Steps:
1. Put the water and sugar into a saucepan and whisk until combined.
2. Add in the berries and lemon juice and zest and put over medium low heat.
3. Mash the berries a bit then whisk the mixture often and let simmer for 15-25 minutes or until a deeply colored, thick sauce forms.
4. Mash the mixture through a mesh strainer to get out excess pulp and seeds.

*Please note this recipe reduces down to only about ⅔-½ cup of liquid….a little goes a long way but double if needed!

Caramel Sauce

Learning to make caramel is for sure a notable memory because it was a very steep uphill climb for me! The first few times I tried it, an eight-year-old setting out to be the best and most technical baker alive, I somehow ended up getting burns on my fingers and a crystallized rock in the saucepan. However, years later, here I am with my own caramel sauce recipe! It took that poor young baker a few tries, but eventually, he succeeded in making multiple different caramel sauce recipes, then pulled together his favorite characteristics from them such as butteriness, heavy caramelization and thick texture to create this one. Even 7 years later, it is still a proud achievement and delicious addition to a cake.

Ingredients:
-2 cups sugar
-6 tbsp salted butter, cut into tablespoon-sized pieces
-2 tbsp heavy cream
-6 tbsp milk

Steps:
1. Pour the sugar into a saucepan and cook over medium high heat, stirring occasionally until melted and amber colored, 10-12 minutes.
2. Take the sugar off the heat and add in the cold butter, piece by piece, whisking to combine.
3. Slowly pour and stir in the milk and cream.
4. Cool before serving.

Chocolate Ganache

My little cousins know this as 'fancy hot fudge', but it is truly so simple yet better than any store-bought fudge sauce you can buy. Whenever I make this, I always catch *at least one* family member eating it by the spoonful before I can use it, which is fine by me because that is truly the sign of a good topping. This recipe is also super easy to make, so the work-reward ratio is through the roof! I wrote this recipe after making and tasting many other ganaches and sort of adjusting it to the preferences of myself and family members, hence, it is a bit more thick than a traditional ganache with more than a one to one chocolate to liquid ratio, and it subs out some cream for milk just to let the chocolate shine even more and not be too heavy.

Ingredients:
-8 oz finely chopped dark chocolate (about 60% cacao)
-5 oz finely chopped milk chocolate
-½ cup milk
-½ cup heavy cream
*Make it mocha! Add 2 ½ tsp of instant powdered espresso to the finished, warm ganache for a delicious coffee flavor

Steps:
1. Pour the chocolate into a large bowl, set aside.
2. Add the cream and milk into either a microwave safe bowl or a small pot and heat over the stove or in the microwave until the mixture begins to bubble.
3. Pour the hot liquid over the chocolate, making sure it is fully covered. Use a towel to cover and let it sit 3-5 minutes.
4. Whisk until the mixture is smooth and thick.

Chocolate Swiss Meringue

In my opinion, the hidden beauty of meringue frosting's sturdiness is that it can stand up to lots of liquid mix ins, such as the large amounts of melted chocolate that make this buttercream a chocoholic's paradise. My mom often describes this as a richer, heavier, more satisfying cousin of a chocolate mousse to justify eating it by the spoonful before I can even get the cake leveled. Still, I can't deny that this stuff is highly addictive and worth the extra work of a meringue-based buttercream, and occasionally I'll join in. Meanwhile, my poor chocolate lab, Duke, looks up at us, puzzled as to why we won't let him lick the mixer. Even he wants some!

Ingredients:
-6 egg whites
-1 ½ cups plus 1 tbsp sugar
-2 sticks (1 cup) salted butter at room temperature
-1/4 cup plus 2 tbsp cocoa powder
-7 oz semisweet chocolate and 3 oz milk chocolate melted and cooled

Steps:
1. Whisk the egg whites and sugar over a double boiler until they become light and foamy and reach a temperature of at least 145 degrees Fahrenheit.
2. Cut the butter into tablespoon sized pieces and add them one by one into the egg white mixture, beating continuously until all the butter is incorporated and the buttercream is light and fluffy.
3. Slowly pour in the melted chocolate and beat until combined.
4. Gently fold in the cocoa powder.

Citrus Cream Cheese Frosting

If it ain't broke, don't fix it. In my (and Duke's) humble opinion, there is almost no way to make a good cream cheese frosting better. Yet, there are always ways to make it different and add a little extra pop of flavor so it compliments a cake even better! Adding citrus to the cream cheese frosting not only adds more alliteration to the name, but it adds even more tang and a nice, zesty flavor that compliments but doesn't overtake the delicious cream cheese flavor.

Ingredients:
-24 oz cream cheese
-1 cup softened salted butter
-3 tbsp reduced orange juice (simmer or microwave until reduced by $\frac{1}{3}$ -$\frac{1}{2}$
-2 tbsp fine orange zest
-5 cups powdered sugar

Steps:
1. In a bowl, combine the butter and cream cheese until a cohesive mixture is formed.
2. Add in the vanilla, orange zest and orange juice and mix until incorporated.
3. Add the powdered sugar cup by cup and mix until smooth, adding milk as needed.

Berry Buttercream

I have never loved to eat just plain American Buttercream, I often find it to be super heavy and sweet. When writing this recipe, countering that with a blast of real berry flavor was the ultimate goal. After a few shots at this recipe and mediocre test batches, I realized that using that little bit of cream cheese (my favorite frosting ingredient) in addition to the butter and reducing the coulis even further could give that light, thick, fluffy texture everyone loves with American buttercream while still getting a fresh, tart berry flavor. Another great bonus of this recipe is that the coulis will dye the buttercream a vibrant, beautiful color that screams "fresh berry." I made this once for my Aunt Barbie's birthday, and everyone knew right away what kind of frosting was on the cake and was ready to dig in!

Ingredients:
- ⅓ cup berry coulis of your choice, highly reduced
- 1 cup salted butter at room temperature
- 2 tbsp heavy cream
- 4 oz cream cheese at room temperature
- 3 cups powdered sugar

Steps:
1. In a bowl, whip the cream cheese and butter until combined.
2. Add in the raspberry coulis and cream and mix until fully incorporated.
3. Add in the powdered sugar cup by cup and whip until it is all incorporated.

Caramel Buttercream

The first time I made this frosting was to ice my dad's **th birthday cake (that is not a typo, he requested I not include his age so the number is censored) since he is one of the biggest caramel fans I know. Therefore, any way I can find to put more caramel into a dessert is good for him! The look on his face when I brought the simple yet elegant cake with caramel buttercream and drips of caramel sauce on top and banana cake in the middle was some of the most joy I've seen him have over food (for a Sloan, that's saying a lot). Seeing that look on people's faces is, for me at least, definitely a reason to continue baking and experimenting to perfect my recipes because the world needs more togetherness and joy which sweets can bring.

Ingredients:

-1 cup salted butter at room temperature
-3 tbsp heavy whipping cream
-2 ½ cups powdered sugar
-½ cup thick caramel sauce of your choice
-1 tsp vanilla extract

Steps:
1. Mix the butter and cream in a bowl until light and fluffy.
2. Add the sugar cup by cup and whip until the mixture is cohesive.
3. Fold in the caramel sauce and vanilla and whip once more.

Coffee Buttercream

At one of my favorite local homemade ice cream shops, Mitchell's, they have the most amazing coffee ice cream. It was Anne's favorite, it's my father's favorite and I have loved it for years even though to this day, as a stressed out high schooler, I still don't really like coffee! While experimenting with proportions of butter to whipped cream and brewed coffee to ground coffee for maximum flavor and texture, I ended up landing on this recipe, and upon tasting it and realizing it tasted like that ice cream base, I put the whisk down and picked a pen up to write this recipe down. Everyone in my family agreed, something that tasted *that* close to ice cream *must* be saved to put on a cake.

Ingredients:
- 1 cup unsalted butter
- 3 ½ cups powdered sugar
- 1 tbsp finely ground instant coffee
- 3 tbsp heavy whipping cream
- 2 tbsp strong brewed espresso

Steps:
1. In a large bowl, slowly add the cream and powdered sugar to the butter and whip until light and fluffy.
2. Gently fold in the coffee powder until fully incorporated.
3. Mix in the espresso until it is fully incorporated and whip once more.

White Chocolate Coconut Buttercream

Living in the Midwestern United States, at least seven out of the twelve months of the year, you're pretty likely going to be cold and wishing for a tropical vacation. To me, the desire for a beach can be quelled a bit by cooking like I'm at the beach and no flavor says beach like that of coconut cream, to which the white chocolate plays a great second fiddle. Subtly sweet and creamy, this is for sure a unique but delicious combo for any coconut lover. The sweetness of the white chocolate and tang of the cream cheese balance out the strong, rich coconut cream and create a thick, satisfying frosting to make any cake a little more like a trip to the beach.

Ingredients:
-1 cup unsalted butter, softened
-4 oz softened cream cheese
-½ cup plus 2 tbsp coconut cream
-2 ½ cups powdered sugar
-1 ¼ tsp vanilla extract
-5 oz white chocolate, melted and cooled

Steps:
1. Whip together the butter, coconut cream and cream cheese until fully combined.
2. Slowly add in the powdered sugar and whip until fully incorporated.
3. Add in the vanilla extract.
4. Gently fold in the white chocolate until fully combined.

Gingerbread Buttercream

Cookie butter and cookies in general are amazing things, especially when put *on* cake. I had always wanted to do something with it (even though just eating it out of the jar is perfectly satisfying on a cheat day), and when I had it spread on ice cream alongside some gingerbread men, I knew I needed my own signature cookie-butter frosting! Increasingly popular among dessert lovers, cookie butter is creamy, sweet and slightly spicy, which makes it the perfect starter or companion for a gingerbread flavor. All the spices in this buttercream amp that flavor up and, combined with the cookie butter, give the frosting a deep, warm flavor to bring back memories of the winter holidays with every bite.

Ingredients:
-½ cup smooth cookie butter
-1 cup salted butter
-2 ½ cups powdered sugar
-2 tbsp milk
-¾ tsp cinnamon
-2 tbsp molasses
-½ tsp ground ginger
 -⅓ tsp ground cloves

Steps:
1. Combine the butter and cookie butter in a bowl and beat until combined.
2. Add in the molasses and spices, whip until incorporated.
3. Add the powdered sugar, a cup at a time and splash in the milk as needed.

Marshmallow Meringue Buttercream

Love them or hate them, marshmallows have a distinct, sticky and fluffy texture and unmistakable flavor that can pair well with so many things to complement its sugary sweetness. As a huge S'mores fan, I knew I had to make some sort of frosting out of it to go on top of chocolate cake with crumbled marshmallows and after lots of sticky messes and flops (let's just say most people don't make homemade marshmallows for a reason), I came up with this. Halfway between a classic meringue and marshmallow fluff, this sturdy, fluffy buttercream has a light, sweet flavor and slightly sticky texture to set it apart from the pack and make you nostalgic for campfires.

Ingredients:
- ½ cup water
- 1 ¼ cup sugar
- ¾ cup corn syrup
- 1 ⅓ tsp vanilla extract
- ⅛ tsp salt
- 5 egg whites
- ⅔ tsp cream of tartar
- 5 tbsp unsalted butter, at room temperature and cut into tablespoon-sized pieces
- ¼ cup powdered sugar

Steps:
1. In a large bowl, whip the egg whites and cream of tartar until soft peaks form.
2. In a small pot, combine your water, sugar, salt and corn syrup and simmer until the temperature reaches 245 degrees Fahrenheit.
3. Slowly pour the hot sugar mixture into the egg whites, whipping as you pour.
4. Whip 12-20 minutes, or until the frosting has completely come to room temperature.
5. Add in the butter, piece by piece, whipping as you go.
6. Add in the powdered sugar and vanilla and whip once more.

Coconut Swiss Meringue

As much as I wish I had some sentimental story about creating this recipe, I really don't...the reason I first made this was pretty simple, I had just gotten my first bottle of coconut extract from Sur La Table and I loved the flavor and smell. Naturally, I wanted to see what desserts I could put it in! I just so happened to be making a cake with vanilla meringue that week, so I took some leftover meringue, added coconut extract and some coconut cream since it gives almost anything a creamy, sweet flavor, and this recipe was an instant success! I always have loved just randomly throwing things together in the kitchen and seeing how it goes, and this is one of those cases where it landed me on one of my favorite frostings to this day!

Ingredients:
-6 egg whites
-15 tbsp unsalted butter, softened and cut into tablespoon-sized pieces
-1 ½ cups sugar
-¼ cup coconut cream
-¼ tsp salt
-1 ½ tsp coconut extract

Steps:
1. Whisk the egg whites, salt, and sugar over a double boiler until they become light and foamy and reach a temperature of at least 145 degrees Fahrenheit.
2. Cut the butter into tablespoon-sized pieces and add them one by one into the egg white mixture, beating continuously until all the butter is incorporated and the buttercream is light and fluffy.
3. Slowly pour in the coconut cream and beat until combined.
4. Mix in the coconut extract.

Custards and Fillings

Vanilla Custard

I guess you could call this my take on a classic pastry cream, but it really was meant to taste like a more flavorful, thick version of an old summer camp-lunch favorite of mine, vanilla pudding. The creamy, sweet taste of this even on its own is like nostalgia mixed with sophistication. Custard like this is such a classic cake filling that it can also be used in so many other desserts and this simple vanilla recipe is for sure a great starting point for learning and mastering the techniques. The process of tempering the egg yolks and cooking them without scrambling them may seem intimidating, but it really just requires LOTS of whisking and attention and maybe a bit of straining afterwards to get a super smooth result.

Ingredients:
-6 egg yolks
-2 ½ cups milk
-½ cup heavy cream
-½ tsp salt
-2 ½ tsp vanilla extract
-⅔ cup sugar

Steps:
1. Whisk the egg yolks, salt and sugar in a large bowl until combined and pale.
2. Pour the milk, cream and vanilla into a saucepan and bring to a simmer over medium high heat.
3. Add 1 cup of the hot milk mixture to the egg yolks, whisking while pouring.
4. Add the rest of the hot milk mixture to the yolk mixture, whisking to combine.
5. Pour the final mixture back into the saucepan and cook over medium low heat until thickened.
6. Chill the custard for 3-4 hours.

Chocolate Custard

On my recipe-creating journey, after I mastered vanilla custard, the next step was obviously to create a chocolate version! My dad, from whom I got my love of pudding, was my taste tester while creating this recipe. And, even though he is rather easy to please with dessert, the two of us agreed that my first iterations, which utilized milk chocolate, were far too sweet and the ones using cocoa powder were not rich enough. The use of the real semisweet chocolate in addition to the cocoa powder and hint of coffee this final recipe gives it a very deep, more dark chocolate-like flavor and dense, rich texture that pairs perfectly with most cakes.

Ingredients:
-7 egg yolks
-3 cups milk
-½ heavy cream
-½ tsp ground coffee
-¾ cup sugar
-10 oz semisweet chocolate, melted
-¼ cup cocoa powder

Steps:
1. Whisk the egg yolks, sugar, coffee, cocoa powder and sugar in a large bowl until combined and pale.
2. Pour the milk and cream into a saucepan and bring to a simmer over medium high heat.
3. Add 1 cup of the hot milk mixture to the egg yolks, whisk while pouring.
4. Add the rest of the hot milk mixture to the yolk mixture, whisking to combine.
5. Pour the final mixture back into the saucepan and cook over medium low heat until thickened.
6. Once thickened (after about 5-10 minutes), pour the custard out into a bowl and fold in the melted chocolate.
7. Cover tightly and chill for 3-4 hours.

Chocolate Mousse

Whenever I make this recipe, I watch the Swedish Chef make chocolate moose (no that is not a spelling error, he uses a moose). My mom and I have always watched classic Muppets clips together whenever we need a laugh and that is by far, one of our favorites. Swedish Chef aside, this recipe, though a bit complicated considering how few ingredients it has, it totally worth a try. It is like whipped cream and chocolate custard combined flavors and textures to make a light and airy, yet flavorful and satisfyingly smooth hybrid.

Ingredients:
-4 eggs, separated plus 1 additional egg white
-6 tbsp sugar
-¼ cup water
-⅓ cup heavy whipping cream
-6 oz semisweet chocolate, melted and cooled

Steps:
1. Over a double boiler, mix the egg whites and 2 tbsp sugar until the mixture reaches 145 degrees Fahrenheit.
2. Take off the heat and whip until stiff peaks form.
3. Over a double boiler but in a separate bowl, combine the egg yolks, water and sugar, and whisk until it reaches 145 degrees Fahrenheit.
4. Take the yolks off the heat and add the melted chocolate, gently fold together.
5. Slowly fold the chocolate and yolk mixture into the whites until combined, then chill 4-6 hours.

Banana Custard

Another banana-flavored item created with my father over our shared love of the sweet, yellow fruit, this custard is taken from a banana ice cream base recipe I wrote trying to recreate Ben and Jerry's Chunky Monkey flavor. Believe it or not, most thicker ice creams and gelatos begin as somewhat of a thinner custard before they are frozen so that transition was rather smooth. That got this custard into cakes and mouths soon after its inception, and I am glad for that!

Ingredients:
- 7 egg yolks
- 2 cups milk
- ¼ cup heavy cream
- ½ tsp salt
- 1 ½ tsp vanilla extract
- ⅔ cup sugar
- 1 ½ medium sized bananas, puréed

Steps:
1. Whisk the egg yolks, salt and sugar in a large bowl until combined and pale.
2. Pour the milk, cream and vanilla into a saucepan and bring to a simmer over medium high heat.
3. Add 1 cup of the hot milk mixture to the egg yolks, whisk while pouring.
4. Add the rest of the hot milk mixture to the yolk mixture, whisking to combine.
5. Pour the final mixture back into the saucepan and cook over medium low heat until thickened.
6. Add the banana purée and cook for 2-3 more minutes.
7. Pour the custard into a large bowl and chill it for 3-4 hours.

Warm Spice Custard

I had never tasted, or even seen a spiced custard prior to this, but, I believe that just because it hasn't been done, doesn't mean it shouldn't be! Of course, sometimes I am wrong in that bold philosophy, but this ended up being a success! Here, I decided to go with a heavier hand on cinnamon with ginger and nutmeg in the background and a little brown sugar for extra sweetness and another warm, spicy bit of flavor. The punchy spices really amp up the mild, sweet custard base and give it a flavor that makes me think of fall in Ohio and its breezy weather that makes pretty much anyone crave apple pie.

Ingredients:
-6 egg yolks
-2 ½ cups milk
-½ cup heavy cream
-¾ tsp nutmeg
-2 tsp cinnamon
-½ tsp ground ginger
-½ cup white sugar
-¼ cup light brown sugar

Steps:
1. Whisk the egg yolks, salt, spices and sugars in a large bowl until combined and pale.
2. Pour the milk, cream and vanilla into a saucepan and bring to a simmer over medium high heat.
3. Add 1 cup of the hot milk mixture to the egg yolks, whisk while pouring.
4. Add the rest of the hot milk mixture to the yolk mixture, whisking to combine.
5. Pour the final mixture back into the saucepan and cook over medium low heat until thickened.
6. Chill the custard for 3-4 hours.

Coconut Custard

This is essentially my take on coconut cream pie filling and do not fret, I brought the coconut flavor! The use of coconut extract and coconut cream gives this not only a smooth texture and powerful coconut flavor, but also a really great, natural sweetness like the fruit itself. Coconut is for sure a love-it-or-hate-it flavor, but when done right, it is almost irresistible and can transport anyone to a beach vacation. For me, it is especially reminiscent of a piña colada-filled winter trip to Cancun I took with my whole extended family. Some of the best kind of food is the kind that brings people together, whether at a table or in spirit and with how many memories it provokes, this recipe for sure does that.

Ingredients:

-¾ cup milk
-¼ cup heavy cream
-1 ¼ cup coconut cream
-½ tsp coconut extract
-½ tsp vanilla extract
-½ cup plus 2 tbsp sugar
-5 egg yolks

Steps:
1. Whisk together the egg yolks and sugar until smooth.
2. Add the milk, cream, coconut milk, coconut extract, and vanilla extract into a small pot and bring to a simmer over medium heat.
3. Add in 1 cup of the hot milk to the egg yolks, whisk while pouring.
4. Slowly add the rest of the milk while whisking.
5. Add the mixture back into the pot and cook over low heat, whisking frequently until thickened.
6. Take the mixture off the heat, pour into a bowl and chill for at least 1 ½ hours.

Fresh Coconut Filling

This takes three out of four elements of coconut cream pie, the cream, coconut flakes and whipped cream and rolls it into one, making it ready to be stuffed into a cake! Even though my chocolate lab, Duke, can't have coconut (or chocolate, ironically), he loves whipped cream, and this recipe came from me making coconut custard and having leftover whipped cream that I made for him as a summer treat. Not that whipped cream on a hot day isn't great, but this is for sure a big step up flavor and texture-wise, with a bit thicker of a consistency and a flavor that can stand on its own or be paired with chocolate, pineapple or others!

Ingredients:
-1 ½ cups coconut custard
-⅔ cup heavy cream
-¾ cup sweetened shredded coconut

Steps:
1. In a large bowl, whip the cream until stiff peaks form.
2. Gently fold in the custard until fully incorporated.
3. Gently fold the coconut into the whipped custard mixture.

Cookies and Cream Custard

After seeing Buddy Valastro, the Cake Boss himself, use cookies and cream filling in a birthday cake for his son, I immediately had to follow suit. The classic combo of chocolate cookies and rich vanilla cream is impeccably delicious on its own and in other desserts, so this was totally a no brainer that I wished I had been making earlier. It took a bit of playing around, but I found that using the white chocolate and cream cheese in the custard base really do make it taste almost like the irresistible cookie centers and the addition of the crushed cookies themselves make this a total favorite of mine.

Ingredients:
-5 egg yolks
-3 oz cream cheese, softened
-2 ½ cups milk
-½ cup heavy cream
-½ tsp salt
-2 tsp vanilla extract
-⅔ cup sugar
-5 oz melted white chocolate
-12 cream-filled cookies, chopped

Steps:
1. Make the vanilla cream custard: whisk the egg yolks, cream cheese, salt and sugar in a large bowl until combined and pale.
2. Pour the milk, cream and vanilla into a saucepan and bring to a simmer over medium high heat.
3. Add 1 cup of the hot milk mixture to the egg yolks, whisk as you pour.
4. Add the rest of the hot milk mixture to the yolk mixture, whisking to combine.
5. Pour the final mixture back into the saucepan and cook over medium low heat until thickened.
6. Whisk the white chocolate into the vanilla custard until fully combined.
7. Fold in the cream-filled cookies.

Lemon Curd

Even though my grandma on my father's side is not a big cook or baker herself, she always wants to know how my baking ventures go and if I can ship her something so she can taste test it. She lives across the country for most of the year, and I enjoy talking to her through texts, emails, phone calls, and even hand written letters. She often jokes that I should slip some cookies into the envelope when we do send the letters! Anyhow, being a pretty sophisticated yet amiable woman herself, it is no surprise that her favorite flavor, lemon, is such a strong, complex one that pairs well with so many things. This filling, my take on a lemon curd and a combination of my favorite recipes from other chefs, with its smooth and rich texture and tart yet sweet flavors, is dedicated to her. The use of zest here is more prominent than in most of the recipes I started with from the internet, but it has my grandma's seal of approval, so it's a keeper.

Ingredients:
-1 ½ cup plus 1 tbsp sugar
-4 eggs plus 1 egg yolk
-½ cup lemon juice
-4 tsp fine lemon zest
-6 tbsp butter, cubed

Steps:
1. Over a double boiler, combine all the ingredients except the butter and whisk vigorously until the mixture becomes paler.
2. Continue to cook the mixture on medium heat, whisking frequently until it reaches 160 degrees Fahrenheit and begins to thicken, about 15-25 minutes.
3. Take off the heat, add the cubes of butter, and whisk until combined. Then, pour into a large bowl and chill for 2-3

Blood Orange Curd

While it sounds a bit crazy and almost eerie, blood orange is actually pretty similar to a regular orange, but even more tart yet sweet and juicy. That, to me, made it a perfect candidate for a curd similar to that traditionally made with lemon. Its smooth texture, strong flavor and bright color make it awesome for crepes, tarts and cakes alike, and though it took few trails, I made it super fresh and fruity, almost like sipping on a glass of fresh squeezed juice.

Ingredients:
- 1 ¼ cup blood orange juice
- ⅔ cup plus 1 tbsp sugar
- 5 egg yolks
- 4 tbsp butter
- 3 tbsp blood orange zest

Steps:
1. In a small bowl, whisk together the egg yolks and sugar until lighter in color and fully combined.
2. Add in the blood orange zest.
3. In a small pot, add the egg yolk mixture to the juice and whisk until combined.
4. Reduce and simmer (do not let come to a full boil), whisking frequently until the mixture has reduced by about ½ and has reached a temperature of at least 165 degrees Fahrenheit.
5. Strain into a bowl and chill for at least 3 hours before serving for best consistency and flavor.

Apple Cake Filling

When writing this recipe, right off the bat, my instinct was to make it taste like putting an apple pie inside a cake. After a bit of experimentation, I found that the best way to do this and make it taste as if the filling was given time to caramelize in the oven is to make almost a caramel sauce out of the sugar and spices before adding the apples. This gives it a thick, syrupy texture and a slightly nutty flavor as if it had been baked and browned that could truly help solve the cake versus pie problem.

Ingredients:
-2 large Granny Smith apples, thinly sliced
-1 large Honeycrisp apples, thinly sliced
-2 tsp lemon juice
-1 tsp lemon zest
-¼ cup plus 1 tbsp light brown sugar
-3 tbsp sugar
-2 tbsp cornstarch
-1 tsp cinnamon
-¼ tsp nutmeg
-¼ tsp ground ginger
-1/3 cup water

Steps:

1. In a saucepot, combine the sugars, lemon juice and zest, water, spices and cornstarch and heat and stir until dissolved and thickened.
2. Turn the heat up to medium and cook 5-10 minutes or until the sugar just begins to turn amber-colored.
3. Pour the liquid over the apples, mixing until fully incorporated.
4. Add the apples back to the pot and cook on low for 5-10 minutes or until softened.
5. Cool before using in a cake.

Peach Cake Filling

As with many things that I taste and love, upon having my first ripe peach of the summer while sitting with my father on a hot day in June, I immediately thought, "I gotta put this in a cake!" A few days later, after waiting for some more peaches to ripen since we'd already eaten the previous bunch, I was on it. After creating the Apple Cake Filling, I'd become experienced at creating fillings for cakes from traditional pie fillings so this one came together pretty well on the first try. The key here is cooking the syrup just enough before putting it on the peaches so that it is sticky but still is able to cook in the pan with the peaches without burning. For this to be possible, the sugar should be dissolved, but the mixture should not have reduced too much.

Ingredients:
-4 peaches, sliced
-¼ cup sugar
- ⅓ cup light brown sugar, packed
-1 tbsp salted butter, melted
-1 tsp lemon juice
-1 tsp lemon zest
-1 tbsp cornstarch
-1 tbsp flour
-¼ tsp cinnamon

Steps:
1. In a small bowl, whisk together the sugars, cinnamon, lemon zest, cornstarch and flour.
2. In a separate larger bowl, add the sliced peaches and set aside.
3. Pour the butter and lemon juice along with 2-3 tbsp water into the sugars and spices.
4. Microwave for 3-5 45 second intervals, stirring in between until the sugar dissolves and the mixture becomes syrupy.
5. Pour the liquid over the peaches and stir to coat everything.
6. Pour the mixture into a saucepot and cook over low heat for 5-10 minutes or until the peaches begin to soften, stirring often.
7. Cool before adding to a cake.

Blackberry-Cherry Cake Filling

Summertime fruits are always delicious, especially in cold Ohio winters when the sun hasn't shown itself fully in days. That's why, with this recipe, my goal was to make something that would work well, even and especially if the fruit was frozen. Frozen cherries and blackberries get packaged and sent to the freezer at the peak of the season, so they taste great and have lots of juice to give up to this thick, tart and sweet cross between and a jam and a coulis. This filling is versatile and super simple, so you can make it for and with almost anyone and anything, it's great for anything from birthdays to barbeques.

Ingredients:
- 1 ½ cups fresh or frozen cherries, pitted and halved
- 1 ¼ cups fresh or frozen blackberries
- ⅓ cup plus 2 tbsp sugar
- 2 tbsp cornstarch
- 1 tbsp lemon juice
- 1 tbsp water

Steps:

1. Put the berries and cherries in a small pot and heat on low until they lose some juice, then add in the water, lemon juice, and cornstarch and stir until fully incorporated with the juices.
2. Turn up the heat a bit and add the sugar, stir until dissolved.
3. Reduce the mixture, simmering on low for 8-12 minutes until it is thickened.
4. Cool before using in a cake.

Dairy Free Coconut Lime Custard

Having allergies to most nuts, peanuts, and legumes has taught me one thing, that it sucks! Not being able to eat sweets and join in on the experiences they are part of is a pretty bad feeling, but it can be avoided since there are so many great substitutes for things like milk, gluten and even eggs! Generally, I like to use regular milk that has had the lactose taken out or soy milk since they have more neutral flavors, but this recipe embraces the slight coconut flavor of coconut milk. In combination with the coconut cream and lime, the coconut is sweet and prominent, a great partner to the zesty lime flavor this custard takes on while it simmers.

Ingredients:
- -1 cup sugar
- - 10 tbsp lime juice
- -1 ½ tbsp lime zest
- -6 egg yolks
- -1 cup coconut cream
- -2 ¼ cups coconut milk

Steps:
1. In a large bowl, whisk together the egg yolks, sugar and lime juice and beat until pale.
2. Combine the coconut milk, lime zest and cream in a pot and heat over medium high heat until simmering.
3. Pour 1 cup of the hot milk mixture into the egg yolks mixture, whisking continuously.
4. Slowly add the rest of the hot milk into the egg mixture, whisk while pouring.
5. Add the mixture back into the pot and cook over medium low heat until thickened (about 15 minutes).

Muffins and Loaves

Basic Banana Bread and Muffins

Simple, classic and delicious any time of the day, a banana bread is always a great recipe to have in your arsenal and a great way to use up overripe bananas. I'm all about reducing food waste whenever possible, especially with the amount of hungry people worldwide and banana bread is probably the best form of food-recycling (or any recycling for that matter) that I know. This recipe is super banana heavy, so most of the sugar is natural, but it also uses both white and brown sugar as well as spices to kick up the flavor just a notch. This is one of those recipes that I find myself making so often that I honestly don't have a specific story or memory to go along with it since, between me and my dad, both banana lovers, the loaf is always gone within a few days.

Ingredients:
-4 ripe bananas, mashed
-4 eggs
-1 cup oil
-½ cup packed brown sugar
-½ cup sugar
-½ cup milk
-2 tsp vanilla extract
-3 cups flour
-2 ¼ tsp baking soda
-1 tsp cinnamon
-½ tsp nutmeg

Steps:
1. In a large bowl, combine the banana, eggs, sugar and oil and beat to combine.
2. Pour in the baking soda, cinnamon and vanilla and mix until fully incorporated.
3. Add ½ of the flour, then then the milk, then the remaining flour, mixing between each step.

4. For a loaf: add the batter to 2 greased 8 inch loaf pans and bake at 350 degrees Fahrenheit for about 50 minutes or until a toothpick inserted into the middle of each loaf comes out clean

   For muffins: divide the batter between 18-20 muffins in greased tins and bake at 350 degrees Fahrenheit for 20-25 minutes or until toothpicks come out clean

Blueberry Muffins

Another classic, blueberry muffins are familiar, recognizable and just delicious! For the first fourteen years of my life, I wouldn't eat blueberries because of their gooey texture, but I would never turn them down all baked up in a muffin, especially one of the muffins from my local grocery store's bakery. Those muffins were just perfectly sweet and moist, and they were absolutely huge! As a little kid, I remember thinking I was such a genius for agreeing to go grocery shopping with my nanny since she would let me get one of these as a reward for 'helping' and frankly, it was definitely worth my patience. These muffins, especially with the optional addition of the large sugar granules for crunch, taste almost exactly like those muffins, and you don't even have to go to the store and do a full shopping trip to get one! The secret to those crispy tops and moist middles is using the combination of my favorite hack, Greek yogurt (or sour cream) and oil in the recipe and baking it at a higher temperature first. The browned, crunchy tops make for an irresistible combo with the soft blueberries inside, so don't be afraid to turn up the heat!

Ingredients:
- ½ cup oil
- ½ tsp salt
- 1 ¼ cup sugar
- 2 eggs
- 2 tsp baking powder
- ½ tsp baking soda
- 2 ½ cups flour
- ¾ cup Greek yogurt or sour cream
- ½ cup milk
- 1 teaspoon vanilla extract
- 2 cups blueberries
- Optional: large granules of sugar for sprinkling on top

Steps:
1. In a large bowl, cream together the eggs and sugar.
2. Slowly pour in the oil while whisking to emulsify.
3. One by one, crack in the eggs and mix between additions.
4. Add in the yogurt or sour cream, vanilla and leaveners and mix to incorporate.
5. Mix in ½ of the flour, then the milk, then the final ½ of the flour.
6. Fold in the blueberries.
7. Pour batter into 18-20 muffin tins slots and bake at 400 degrees Fahrenheit for 10-15 minutes or until risen and browned but not cooked through.
   If using the large granule sugar, quickly sprinkle atop the muffins now

8. Turn the oven temperature down to 325 degrees Fahrenheit and bake another 5-10 minutes or until a toothpick inserted into the center of a muffin comes out dry.

Chocolate Protein Blender Muffins

The bodybuilder side of me couldn't bear to write a whole cookbook without an anabolic, protein-packed recipe so here you go! Never fear, this one is super nutritious with whole grains, tons of protein (11 grams!) and very low sugar and fat, yet the muffins are super tasty! With a great macronutrient profile, they can easily fit into anybody's day for a mid-afternoon energy boost or even a 125 calorie breakfast (so you can eat more dessert later guilt free), I always choose to have them for a post-workout afternoon snack with come fruit, and they give me the energy I need to power through until dinner. On top of all the deliciousness and nutrition they provide, they are incredibly easy to make, the blender is an awesome tool here to only to mix the batter, but pulverize the oats into more of a flour so the batter is more smooth like a traditional muffin.

Ingredients:
-2 cups oats
-3 eggs
-8 tbsp cocoa powder
-4 heaping scoops chocolate whey protein powder
-16 oz vanilla non-fat Greek yogurt
-2 ¼ tsp baking powder
-1 cup water

Steps:
1. Put the oats, protein powder, baking powder and cocoa into a blender, blitz until the oats are broken down into a flour-like powder.
2. Add in all the wet ingredients and blend again until the mixture is smooth and everything is incorporated well.
3. Divide the batter into 15 greased muffin tins and bake at 350 degrees Fahrenheit for 20-25 minutes.

Dark Chocolate Banana Bread

Easily two of the best dessert flavors on the planet, chocolate and banana, are amazing apart, but in this bread, they are off the charts together! This one is sort of a mash up of two of my favorite desserts: chocolate cake and banana bread, and it for sure can satisfy all of my cravings. Getting the balance of chocolate to banana can be more difficult than expected since they both can be such dominant flavors, but having many failed (but still super tasty, lol) trails of this recipe were worth it for the resulting moist, chocolatey loaf with a strong flavor of banana.

Ingredients:
-2 ½ large bananas, mashed
-1 ¼ cup plus all-purpose flour or oat flour
-⅔ cup cocoa powder
-¾ cup sugar
-⅓ cup light brown sugar
-2 eggs
-¾ cup melted salted butter
-1 teaspoon vanilla extract
-⅔ cup Greek yogurt
-3 tsp baking powder
-½ tsp baking soda
-1 cup chocolate chips, if desired

Steps:
1. In a bowl, whisk together the eggs, bananas and sugars.
2. Slowly add in the melted butter and whisk to fully combine.
3. Add in the Greek yogurt, baking powder and vanilla and whisk again until fully incorporated.
4. Fold in the flour and cocoa powder until they are fully incorporated and the batter is smooth.
5. Optional: stir in the chocolate chips.
6. Pour the batter into a greased and floured 9-inch square pan and bake at 350 degrees Fahrenheit for 40-50 minutes or until a toothpick comes out clean.

Cinnamon Roll Bread or Muffins

Probably one of the most delicious and iconic morning time or anytime treats of all time, the cinnamon roll is for sure a favorite pastry dessert of mine. There are quite a few bakeries around my house that make them, and if I'm having a breakfast cheat meal, they are an absolute must! After craving a cinnamon roll that I could bake fresh anytime without dealing with the stress and cleanup of a yeasted dough, I decided on creating a quick loaf version. I aimed to make the base batter itself here almost a cross between a bread dough and a muffin batter and the cinnamon swirl is about as close to the filling of real cinnamon rolls as it gets, so the resulting loaf is basically a giant, sliceable cinnamon roll! It's best served fresh out of the oven with the cream cheese glaze for the icing on the cinnamon roll, and it is irresistible any time of day.

Ingredients:

Base batter:
-2 eggs
-1 cup sugar
-½ cup salted butter
-1 ½ tsp vanilla extract
-1 cup milk
-3 tsp baking powder
-2 3/4 cups flour

Cinnamon swirl:
-5 tsp cinnamon
-3 tbsp sugar
-3 tbsp brown sugar
-¼ cup milk

Glaze:
- 6 oz cream cheese, room temperature
-2 oz salted butter at room temperature
-1 cup plus 2 tbsp powdered sugar
-1 ½ tsp vanilla extract
-¼ cup milk

Steps:
1. In a large bowl, beat together the butter and sugar until smooth and light.
2. Add in the eggs one by one, beating to incorporate.
3. Add in the vanilla and baking powder and mix to combine.

4. Alternate adding ½ of the flour, the milk, and then the other ½ of the flour, mixing between each step.
5. In a separate small bowl, add together the cinnamon, sugars, and milk and whisk to form a thick paste, add more milk if the mixture is too dry.

For muffins:
6. Divide ½ of the batter between 12 greased muffin tins and then add some of the cinnamon sugar paste into each and swirl with a toothpick, repeat with the rest of the batter and cinnamon sugar paste.
7. Bake at 350 degrees Fahrenheit for 20-25 minutes.

For a loaf:

6. Pour the ½ of the batter into a 10 inch loaf pan then add ½ of the cinnamon sugar paste and swirl with a toothpick, then repeat the process.

7. Bake at 350 degrees Fahrenheit for about 50-55 minutes or until a toothpick inserted into the middle of the loaf comes out clean.

Glaze:
1. Add the butter and cream cheese to a bowl and beat to combine.
2. Slowly add the powdered sugar and mix until incorporated.
3. Add in the vanilla and milk and mix until the mixture is thin enough to pour.
4. Drizzle or spread the glaze atop the loaf cakes or muffins. If you have made muffins, dipping the tops into the glaze also works very well!.

Orange Chocolate Chip Muffins

Citrus and chocolate have always seemed like sort of an unlikely pairing to me, but they normally end up tasting even more awesome together than apart! I was inspired to write this recipe after falling in love with the combo from eating a chocolate covered orange peel and wanting to give the choco-citrus flavor the recognition it deserves! The name of the game here was zesty, tangy, and sweet and the use of zest as well as the juice of the orange and buttermilk ensures that the flavor is there and not overpowered by the chocolate chips. Orange may not seem like a typical cake/muffin flavor, but making this recipe made a believer out of me, I hope it does for you too.

Ingredients:
-½ cup freshly squeezed orange juice
-1 heaping tablespoon finely grated orange zest
-¾ cup sugar
-2 eggs
-1 cup buttermilk
-½ cup salted butter
-3 tsp baking powder
-2 ¼ cups flour
-1.5-2 cups semisweet chocolate chips

Steps:
1. In a large bowl, cream together the butter and sugar.
2. One by one, add the eggs, mixing the batter until the egg is incorporated each time.
3. Add in the orange juice, zest and baking powder and mix until combined.
4. Add in ½ of the flour, then the buttermilk, then the remaining flour, mixing between each stage.
5. Fold in the chocolate chips.
6. Divide the batter between 18-20 greased muffin tins and bake at 350 degrees Fahrenheit for about 20 minutes.

Apple Cinnamon Swirl Cake

This cake has totally become a family tradition, I have made this one at least six times this year for barbeques, Jewish High Holidays, Thanksgiving, Super Bowl, and casual dinners (because cake doesn't need a special occasion). It's great because it satisfies cinnamon roll, cake, and apple pie cravings in one fell swoop, and it has a pretty gentle warm spice flavor that almost anyone in a crowd will like. Apple-cinnamon is probably on my list of top flavor combos, so making a cake dedicated to it was a priority when I went on a recipe writing rampage. Rest assured, this one, though a big unique in its process, has come out of the oven delicious and moist from day one.

Ingredients:

Batter:
-2 apples, diced into ⅓ inch cubes
-3 ¼ cups flour
-3 eggs
-1 cup vegetable oil
-1 ½ tbsp lemon juice
-1 cup light brown sugar
-⅔ cup sugar
-1 ¼ tsp cinnamon
-½ tsp ground ginger
-½ tsp ground nutmeg
-¼ tsp ground mace
-¾ cup milk
-2 tsp baking powder
-1 tsp baking soda

Cinnamon Swirl:
-6 tbsp melted salted butter
-¼ cup light brown sugar
-¼ cup sugar
-1 tbsp cinnamon

Steps:
1. Combine the eggs and sugars in a bowl and beat until light and fluffy.
2. Add the oil slowly and beat until fully incorporated.
3. Add in the lemon juice, spices, baking powder and baking soda and mix until combined.
4. Add in ⅓ of the flour, then ½ of the milk and repeat this until all the flour and milk are incorporated, mixing in between each step.

5. Fold in the apples.
6. In a separate bowl, mix together the melted butter, sugars and cinnamon and put into a piping bag.
7. Divide ⅓ of the cake batter into 2 greased 8-inch loaf pans.
8. Add in stripes of the cinnamon sugar mixture and use a toothpick to swirl
9. Repeat steps 7 and 8.
10. Bake at 350 degrees for about 45-50 minutes or until a toothpick comes out clean from the middle of the cake.

Lemon Blueberry Loaf

The flavor of this pound cake-like loaf is sweet, tart, fresh and tangy. The lemon juice and zest combined with sour cream or Greek yogurt and buttermilk keep the cake incredibly moist and make it not-too sweet while the fresh blueberries add some texture and extra sweet flavor. The combo of the two fruits for sure is a classic, but some of the extra nuances here make this recipe yet another special one perfect for gathering around the table and eating with loved ones.

Ingredients:
-2 cups fresh blueberries
-⅓ cup plus 1 ½ tsp lemon juice
-4 tsp finely grated lemon zest
-2 cups sugar
-1 cup sour cream or Greek yogurt
-½ cup oil
-⅔ cup buttermilk
-3 eggs
-2 ¾ cup plus 1 tbsp flour
-1 ½ tsp baking powder
-⅓ tsp baking soda
-½ tsp salt

Steps:
1. In a small bowl, toss the blueberries in 1 tbsp of flour.
2. In a separate bowl, cream the eggs and sugar until light and fluffy.
3. Add in the sour cream and beat once more.
4. Slowly pour in the oil and mix to emulsify.
5. Add in the vanilla, baking powder, baking soda and lemon zest and mix until incorporated.
6. Add in ⅓ of the flour, followed by the lemon juice, then another ⅓ of the flour, followed by the milk, then the rest of the flour and mix until incorporated in between each step
7. Fold in the blueberries.
8. Pour the batter into 2 greased 8-inch loaf pans and bake at 350 degrees for 45-50 minutes.

Honey Almond Cornbread

Fun fact about me, I am allergic to peanuts, and all other nuts except almonds! When we first found this out from an allergy test, I was pretty ecstatic, and to this day, almonds are one of my favorite additions for a nutty, textural element in desserts and savory dishes alike. Cornbread has always been something I've enjoyed, especially alongside some good barbeque and with a bit of honey butter, and its unique crumb interested me. When it came time to write this book and I was looking to create a few more unique recipes, the idea of a honey sweetened cornbread with toasty almonds popped into my mind, and I'm sure glad it did! These muffins have a unique sweetness from the honey, nuttiness and crunch from the almonds, and a slightly flaky, moist crumb that makes the baked treats savory, sweet and satisfying.

Ingredients:

-1 ⅓ cups cornmeal
-1 ¼ cup flour
-½ cup honey
-¼ cup plus 1 tbsp sugar
-9 oz buttermilk
-⅓ cup oil
-2 eggs
-½ tsp salt
-1 ¼ cups chopped almonds
-2 tsp baking powder

Steps:

1. Spread out the almonds on a baking sheet and toast 5-10 minutes at 375 degrees Fahrenheit, set aside to cool.
2. Combine the eggs, honey, sugar, oil and buttermilk in a large bowl and whisk together.
3. Add in the cornmeal, flour, baking powder, and salt (start with about half of the cornmeal and flour, then mix and add the rest) and mix until just combined.
4. Fold in the toasted almonds.
5. Divide between 18-20 greased muffin tins and bake at 350 degrees Fahrenheit for 20-25 minutes.

Oat, Maple, and Chia Muffins

As a younger kid, I actually had some pretty bad sensory processing issues, because of them, I **hated** certain foods, one of them being oatmeal, only because of texture. One of the ways I first incorporated oats into my diet before I overcame my texture issues was to make baked oats with my mom. This recipe is essentially a cross between baked oats and a normal muffin, and the addition of maple and chia adds both awesome flavor and some nice texture and omega 3s, too. The spices and maple pair really well together and, combined with some good toppings, give these oat-packed muffins a really kicked up flavor and texture that proves oatmeal doesn't have to be boring or bland.

Ingredients:
-4 eggs
-1 cup milk
-6 tbsp melted coconut oil or butter
-1 cup Greek yogurt
-⅔ cup maple syrup
-¼ cup brown sugar
-1 tbsp molasses
-1 tsp vanilla extract
-1 ¼ tsp cinnamon
-½ tsp nutmeg
-½ tsp ginger
-2 tbsp chia seeds
-2 ½ cups rolled oats
-1 ¼ cup flour
-2 tsp baking powder
-¾ tsp baking soda
-2 cups dried cranberries, raisins, chopped nuts, or other add-ins

Steps:
1. In a large bowl, whisk together the eggs, sugar and maple syrup until combined.
2. Slowly pour in the coconut oil/butter and whisk to emulsify.
3. Pour in the greek yogurt, vanilla, spices, chia seeds, baking soda and powder, and molasses and whisk to combine.
4. Add in the half of the flour and oats, then half of the milk, repeating and whisking between each addition.
5. Gently fold in the chia seeds and and other add-ins (if desired).

6. Divide into 20-24 greased muffin tins and bake at 350 degrees Fahrenheit for 20-25 minutes.

Brown Butter Pound Cake

When I was younger and someone mentioned brown butter in a dish, I would instantly be super impressed, and when I tasted brown butter cookies for the first time, I was shocked at how rich and nutty they were…little did I know how simple brown butter is to make! Since then, I have put the stuff in so many things, from pasta sauces to cookies to a glaze for some fish and beyond! All you need to do is slightly toast the milk solids in butter, and it goes from a mild, basic ingredient to a toasty, rich blast of flavor. I've always loved pound cake for its simplicity and satisfying density, so upon discovering the wonders of brown butter, the two seemed like a perfect match. The slight saltiness and nuttiness of the butter and the subtle vanilla flavor and sweetness of pound cake create a pretty upscale tasting version of the classic loaf that is awesome for bringing to a party, brunch, or other gathering to bring the people you care about together.

Ingredients:
- 1 ¼ cups salted butter, cubed
- 1 tbsp vanilla extract
- 5 eggs
- ½ cup sour cream or Greek yogurt
- 2 ½ cups sugar
- 2 tsp baking soda
- 3 ½ cups flour

Steps:
1. In a small saucepan, melt the butter on low heat, then turn the heat up to medium and cook the butter, stirring occasionally until the milk solids begin to brown.
2. Pull the butter off the heat and add 2-3 ice cubes to stop the cooking and prevent burning.
3. In a large bowl, cream together the eggs and sugar until light and fluffy.
4. Add in the yogurt/sour cream, vanilla and baking soda and mix to incorporate.
5. Slowly add in the butter, mixing to blend it in.
6. Gently fold in the flour until the batter is cohesive.
7. Divide the batter between 2 greased 8-inch loaf pans and bake at 350 degrees Fahrenheit for about 55 minutes to an hour.

Banana Piña Colada Bread

Something about the sweetness of bananas, the creaminess of coconut and the tartness of fresh pineapple makes this combo absolute dynamite! The inspiration for this came from a workout recovery smoothie I made to carb up after a hard leg day that included frozen bananas and pineapples and was blended with some protein powder and coconut milk since that was what we had on hand and it was unexpectedly delicious. So much so, that I was *almost* wanting to repeat leg day to drink it again. The combo, sure enough, was even more delicious with some butter, sugar and flour thrown in and baked, and this tropical treat is a hit with both banana bread and piña colada loves alike.

Ingredients:
- 3 ripe bananas
- 3 eggs
- 2 ¼ cups flour
- 1 ¼ tsp baking powder
- ½ tsp baking soda
- ½ cup sugar
- ½ cup light brown sugar
- ½ cup sweetened shredded coconut
- ¼ cup pineapple juice, reduced slightly by microwave
- ¼ cup coconut cream
- ¾ cup vegetable oil
- 1 tsp allspice
- ⅔ cup pineapple, diced into ⅛ inch cubes

Steps:
1. In a bowl, mash the bananas until only very small chunks remain or until smooth.
2. Add in the eggs and whisk until incorporated.
3. Add in the sugar and oil and mix until combined.
4. Add in the coconut cream and pineapple juice and mix once more.
5. Fold in the flour, baking powder and baking soda until combined.
6. Gently fold in the chopped pineapple and shredded coconut.
7. Pour the batter into a greased 5 by 9 inch loaf pan and bake at 350 degrees Fahrenheit for about 60 minutes or until a toothpick inserted deep into the center comes out clean.

Nut Butter and Jelly Muffins

An almond butter or sunflower butter and jelly sandwich has been one of my favorite snacks since I was really little! Nothing beats the salty, nutty, satisfying flavor of nut butter combined with some sweet, fruity jelly, and sandwiches are such an easy thing to make and eat on the go. These muffins are all that and more, with a slightly sweet, moist yet crumbly base and a bit of still gooey jelly in the center. To me, they taste super nostalgic, like days at summer camp and hikes in the woods, and they have always been a hit with kids from the neighborhood or my younger cousins.

Ingredients:
-2 ⅔ cups all-purpose flour
-¾ cup sugar
-½ cup light brown sugar
-1 cup water
-3 eggs
-½ cup salted butter
-¾ cup smooth nut butter of choice
-1 cup milk
-1 tsp vanilla extract
-1 tsp cinnamon
-1 ½ tsp baking soda
-1 tsp baking powder
- ⅔ cup jam or jelly of choice

Steps:
1. In a pot over low heat, combine the water, nut butter and butter and stir until melted together and combined then cool.
2. In a bowl, beat together the eggs and sugars until light in color and smooth.
3. Pour cooled nut butter mixture into the eggs and sugar and mix until combined.
4. Add in the vanilla, salt, baking powder and baking soda and mix well.
5. Add in half of the flour, then the milk, then the remaining flour, mixing after each step until just combined.
6. Divide half of the batter between 20-24 greased muffin tins, add about ½-1 tablespoon of jelly or jam into each muffin and top with the remaining batter.
7. Bake at 350 degrees Fahrenheit for about 20-25 minutes or until a toothpick comes out clean

Strawberry Shortcake Muffins

After making the Nut Butter and Jelly Muffins, I knew I had to turn another classic sweet food into an all-encompassing, easy to eat muffin! The muffin base here is reminiscent of biscuits, swapping regular milk for buttermilk for a rich, tangy flavor and slightly flaky crumb. The fresh strawberries, though not a typical muffin mix-in, add a nice tart-sweet balance and a bit of texture to each bite which makes the whole thing reminiscent of real strawberry shortcake. These are super simple and a bit unconventional, yet so delicious that blueberry muffins might have something coming their way!

Ingredients:
-1 cup buttermilk
-3 eggs
-½ cup salted butter
-¾ cup plus 2 tbsp sugar
-2 tsp vanilla extract
-2 ½ tsp baking powder
-2 ½ cups flour
-2 cups fresh, chopped strawberries
-2 tbsp cornstarch

Steps:
1. In a large bowl, cream the sugar and butter.
2. Add in the eggs one by one, mixing after each egg is added.
3. Add the the baking powder and vanilla and mix to combine.
4. Alternate adding ⅓ of the flour then ½ of the buttermilk and mixing to incorporate.
5. In a separate small bowl, sprinkle the cornstarch over the strawberries and lightly coat them to prevent sinking.
6. Fold the strawberries into the batter.
7. Divide the batter between 18-20 greased muffin tins and bake at 350 degrees Fahrenheit for 20-25 minutes.

Natural Zucchini Muffins

Don't be fooled by the lack of flour, butter or sugar in these, they taste awesome! Most zucchini bread is so deceivingly unhealthy because it has vegetables, yet it is often loaded with sugar and fat! So, yes, you get the small amount of veggies, but you get a whole lot of other stuff with it. These muffins have the zucchini in them and they have a slightly spiced, sweet, nutty flavor and tons of moisture, but they also have hidden protein from the heavy hand on eggs, the Greek yogurt, and the almond flour. Fiber is also a key party of a healthy diet and great for staying full, and these muffins pack that in, too. In other terms, they are pretty much one of those health toasts or bowls you might get for a hugely ramped up price at some fancy coffee shop, but these are portable, easy to make and actually taste good!

Ingredients:

-1 large zucchini, grated and excess water squeezed out
-½ cup honey or maple syrup plus 2 tbsp
-4 eggs
-½ cup Greek yogurt
-1 ⅓ cups almond flour
-¾ cup oat flour
-1 tsp vanilla
-1 ¼ tsp cinnamon
-½ tsp nutmeg
-2 tbsp baking soda

Steps:
1. In a large bowl, combine the honey/maple syrup, vanilla, eggs and yogurt together.
2. Fold in the cinnamon, nutmeg, flours and baking soda until the mixture is smooth and combined.
3. Gently fold in the zucchini and any other desired mix-ins
4. Divide the batter into 12-15 muffins in greased muffin tins and bake at 350 degrees Farenheit for about 20 minutes.

Pumpkin Bread with Pumpkin Seed Streusel

It's pretty hard to beat a warm slice of pumpkin bread fresh from the oven, especially in the breezy Ohio falls or after a hard workout in my cool basement! This recipe goes beyond just an awesome loaf though, the streusel topping is sweet, salty, and crunchy and adds just enough to this pumpkin bread to step it up without it losing its true flavor. Pumpkin seeds are always a great little snack with a unique flavor and adding them to a recipe was a must for me, and the sweetness of the streusel helps them blend right into this recipe atop plenty of real pumpkin in the moist, satisfying loaf.

Ingredients:

Bread:
- 15 oz pumpkin purée
- 3 cups all-purpose flour
- 1 cup sugar
- ⅔ cup packed light brown sugar
- 4 eggs
- 1 cup vegetable oil
- ⅓ cup milk
- 1 ½ tsp baking powder
- 1 ½ tsp baking soda
- 2 ½ tsp cinnamon
- 1 ¼ tsp nutmeg
- ½ tsp ground cloves
- ¾ tsp ground ginger

Streusel:
- ½ cup chopped pumpkin seeds
- ¼ cup plus 1 tablespoon brown sugar
- ⅓ cup oats
- ¼ cup flour
- 6 tbsp cold salted butter, cubed
- ½ tsp cinnamon
- ¼ tsp ginger

Steps:
1. In a large bowl, combine the oil, sugars and eggs and beat until smooth.
2. Add in the spices, pumpkin and leaveners and mix again.
3. Add in 2 cups of flour and mix to combine.

4. Add in the milk and mix again.
5. Add in the remaining flour and mix until fully incorporated
6. Make the streusel: add all the dry ingredients into a small bowl and mix, then add the small cubes of butter and incorporate them by hand until the mixture forms small clumps
7. Pour the batter into 2 greased 8 by 4 inch loaf pans and top each loaf with the streusel and lightly pack down.
8. Bake at 350 degrees Fahrenheit for around 50 minutes to an hour or until a toothpick comes out clean.

Favorite Cake Combos

While the intention behind separating cake, frosting, and filling recipes in this book was to allow for the readers to be creative and customize their cakes to their likes and dislikes, here are some fun suggestions of combinations that many people wouldn't consider to get you started.

The Bad Apple: Chocolate Spice Cake with Apple Filling and either Vanilla American Buttercream, Vanilla Swiss Meringue, or Cream Cheese Frosting---This cake is sweet, warm, and a touch spicy! The spices in the cake and filling and the richness of the chocolate balance super well with the tangy, fresh apples and make for a sweet, complex treat!

A Bite of The Beach: Pineapple cake with Blood Orange Curd and Marshmallow Meringue or Cream Cheese Frosting---Pineapple and Orange are always a winning combo in my book, their sweet and tart flavors are always refreshing and delicious, whether in a drink at the beach or in a cake.

When Life Gives You Lemons: Lemon Cake with Lemon Curd and Vanilla Swiss Meringue--- This one's for all the lemon lovers out there! Lots of sweet, tangy, and tart flavor with a super light, mild frosting to bring it all together, this cake is great for summertime,

Thanksgiving in December: Carrot Cake with Warm Spice Custard and Gingerbread Buttercream---Carrot Cake is probably one of the most delicious and iconic Thanksgiving desserts, at least in my family. It is often made with Cream Cheese Frosting, but if you want to take things up a notch and add some Christmas flavor in, the Gingerbread Buttercream combo is for you.

Just Peachy: Almond or Vanilla Cake with Peach Filling, Caramel and Cream Cheese Frosting---This cake is sweet, fresh, nutty, and tangy, a fully loaded combo of flavors that is sure to please both the dessert traditionalists and the adventurous.

The Identity Crisis: Marble Cake with Vanilla Custard, Whipped Chocolate Frosting, and Chocolate Ganache---The age old question: Chocolate or Vanilla? Which is this cake?! Both!

Nuts for The Tropics: Banana Cake with Coconut Custard or Fresh Coconut Filling and Citrus Cream Cheese Frosting---A special twist on the classic banana cake, this combo adds the subtle sweetness or coconut and the tart punch of orange, it is 3 fruits in one and super delicious.

Chocolate-Berry Cloud: Angel Food Cake with Chocolate Mousse and Berry Buttercream--- This cake brings the delicious, intense flavors of berry and chocolate to new heights by placing them in with the light, mild angel food cake.

The Sticky Jack-O-Lantern: Pumpkin Cake with Chocolate Ganache and Caramel Buttercream---Combining the candy flavors of Halloween with the pumpkins is kind of a no brainer here, the spices play super well off the caramel and the ganache never hurts anything!

Anne's Favorite: Chocolate Cake with Chocolate Custard, Ganache and Coffee Buttercream (often served with coffee ice cream) --- Last, but not least, on the list of favorite combos is the cake that I made for Anne on Christmas, when she and Ana celebrated their wedding vows, and on her birthday. It may be the classic combo of chocolate and coffee, but my memories associated with it make it absolutely unforgettable for me and a notable addition to this list.

About the Author

Chase Sloan is a fifteen-year-old aspiring surgical oncologist (cancer surgeon), bodybuilder, and avid chef/baker from Cleveland, Ohio. He lives with his mother, who is a medical researcher and professor, and his father, who is an accomplished neurosurgeon and chocolate lab, Duke, who is just a "really good boy." In his free time, he enjoys spending time with family and friends, lifting weights in his home gym, volunteering at local organizations, exploring outdoors, and experimenting in the kitchen since he has always loved to bring joy to others through baked goods. The thrill of experimenting in the kitchen has led him to write many recipes which he has tweaked through trial and error over the years, and to this day, he still creates and tests new ones when inspiration strikes. Being surrounded by medical professionals and being interested in philanthropy lead him to want to make a difference in the many lives impacted by cancer, even though, being a teenager, he can't physically treat it at the moment. Bodybuilding has taught him to seize opportunity and work hard to achieve his goals, so he decided to use the extra time he had due to cancelled plans from the Covid-19 pandemic to finally achieve a long-time goal of writing a cookbook to raise some money for the cause. This book is a compilation of all the original cake-related recipes he has written over his years of baking and experimenting in the kitchen, which have brought joy to him and many others over his years of baking.

Acknowledgements

I would like to thank……

My mother and father, for teaching me the importance of both hard work and philanthropy, and for supporting and loving me through the ups and downs of numerous hours in front of the computer and messes in the kitchen it took to write this book

Mrs. Leslie Coleman, for being the most hilarious, yet thorough, English teacher and editor ever

Lizzie Kasubick for being a great friend as well as an incredibly talented artist and creating the cover art

Ana Maldonado, for her support and encouragement in my life as a whole, and especially for taste-testing during the book writing process

Anne Duli, for inspiring me to keep fighting for my dreams and to always help others along the way - may she rest in peace

Made in the USA
Coppell, TX
12 September 2020